FIFTEEN MILES
The Wisdom of an Adopted Son

PAUL MAINVILLE

Fifteen Miles. Copyright © 2019 Paul Mainville. Produced and printed by Stillwater River Publications. All rights reserved. Written and produced in the United States of America. This book may not be reproduced or sold in any form without the expressed, written permission of the authors and publisher.

Visit our website at **www.StillwaterPress.com** for more information.

First Stillwater River Publications Edition

Library of Congress Control Number: 2019917512

ISBN: 978-1-950339-53-2

1 2 3 4 5 6 7 8 9 10
Written by Paul Mainville
Cover illustration by Michael J. Wackell, Sr. *www.SouthPawWatercolors.com*
Published by Stillwater River Publications, Pawtucket, RI, USA.

Publisher's Cataloging-In-Publication Data
(Prepared by The Donohue Group, Inc.)

Names: Mainville, Paul, author.
Title: Fifteen miles : the wisdom of an adopted son / Paul Mainville.
Description: First Stillwater River Publications edition. | Pawtucket, RI, USA : Stillwater River Publications, [2019]
Identifiers: ISBN 9781950339532
Subjects: LCSH: Mainville, Paul. | Adopted children--Biography. | Foster children--Biography. | Identity (Psychology) | Self-realization. | LCGFT: Autobiographies.
Classification: LCC HV874.82.M35 A3 2019 | DDC 362.734092 B--dc23

The views and opinions expressed in this book are solely those of the author and do not necessarily reflect the views and opinions of the publisher.

Dedication

*I would like to thank
my Mom and Dad, Ernest and Lucille Mainville,
my brother Peter, and all my relatives for being my family.*

*I would like to recognize Marilyn Lace Johnson
for having the courage to send me to a better place.
Saying that—a better place—will always make me question
the reality of that statement.*

*I would also like to thank AJ, Ellen, and Elizabeth
and their children for making me feel welcome to my other family.*

*Thank you to Samantha Konan
for helping me with the title of this book.*

*Special thanks to my sweetheart Jodi
for taking a stack of paper and creating my original manuscript.
This is when my book became real!*

*And untold thanks to Steve Porter,
owner of Stillwater Publications,
for whose guidance I am truly appreciative.*

*This book represents the journey
and story of Paul Michael Mainville.*

Prologue

Dear Reader,

My life has been such that many people have said, "Mainville, you need to write this stuff down." So here it is. It is not a sunshine and flowers kind of a story but more a tale of a life hidden behind the unknown. It is my story of the trials and tribulations of understanding who, what, when, where, and why I believed that, all my life, I wasn't good enough.

As I searched for tales like mine, I don't see any told the way I wanted to tell it. For the few people who are aware of my story and my attempts to bring it to fruition, their comments have been, "Paul, you need to do this."

This story was written so that children and adults will hopefully be able to gain a better understanding of what it feels like to grow up adopted or as a foster child. This story is sometimes embarrassing, but it is wrapped in humility and possesses my sincere hope that my struggles will help others avoid the same mistakes. It has been a long process as my typing skills are non-existent (thank goodness for voice recognition software!) and there is just so much to tell. I've read, reread, and rewritten this story several times.

"*....Ring, ring, ring and then a woman answered the phone. Thinking that she had died, I asked for Mr. Johnson. The woman* *answering the phone hesitated before saying, "I'm sorry but Mr. Johnson has passed away. I am Mrs. Johnson. Is there something I can help you with?" At that moment I realized that I could be speaking to the woman that I had wondered about my entire life..."*

My name is Paul Mainville, and as you will see in this book, I am not a complex person. I've never written a book, and the only real experience I have is the butt-kickin' I have taken along life's road. I pray that what He has told me to do will come to fruition with your help. I'm a simple man and a roofing contractor by trade, but that is just a smidgen of my life. So now let me tell you the rest of the story.

Sincerely,

Paul Michael Mainville
Father, Grandfather, Business Owner, Martial Arts Student, Student of Native American Tradition, and Son of the Most High God

CHAPTER ONE
Family

I remember a hot summer day many years ago. I was a young man working on a job installing some rolled roofing on the porch of an old house in Pascoag, Rhode Island. I recall working shirtless in the midday sunshine, getting a free tan, and letting the sweat bead and roll down my back. The work was exhausting, and I wished I was somewhere else in the world—anywhere else—at that moment. In the main house attached to the porch, I noticed a girl looking back at me from inside her bedroom window. She had curly hair, big eyes, and a bright smile. She opened her window and we started to talk as I worked, and I immediately felt a connection. The conversation was easy, and my mind wandered. I began to think about walking off the job and hopping through her window and...

I just needed the money too badly. It would be many years before I truly understood how important that seemingly innocent moment would be.

In the small industrial city of Woonsocket, Rhode Island sometime in 1955, Ernie and Lucille Mainville decided to adopt a child. As fate would have it, my parents were unable to conceive. Ernie had a low sperm count and so pregnancy was not a possibility. Lucky for me, they decided to adopt. Years later my Aunt Theresa would say that my Mom, who was a redhead, asked the nuns at the orphanage if there was a redheaded baby boy available. And there I lay—a little bundle of red-haired joy!

My life started out, for all appearance's sake, like that of any other baby. Mom and Dad took great care of me the way any proud parents would care for a child. They took me home the same way any parents might come home with their newborn baby. My life began the way any child's would—or so it seemed. Years later I would come to realize that this was not quite true.

I do have one youthful recollection. I recall my mother coming into my room every night to take care of me. You see, the few months that I was in the orphanage, I had laid mostly on my back and the back of my head had become flat. When my mom put me to bed at night, she would lay me on my stomach and tuck the blankets in very tight around me so that I could not turn over onto my back. Then in the middle of the night, every night, she would come into my room, flip on the overhead light, and check to make sure that I had not rolled over. If I had, she would flip me back onto my stomach and tuck the blankets in tightly again. I think my Mom did this for many months, but I'm not sure exactly how long. It's funny how you can recall certain things.

When I was almost three years old, my brother Peter arrived on the scene. Peter was also adopted, and we would grow up as brothers. I can still remember Peter's first birthday and his fascination with the lone candle on his birthday cake. Filled with great curiosity, he decided he wanted to touch the flame. I remember the look on his face, to this day, when his finger met the fire. OUCH! His face scrunched and tears flowed as his brain registered the pain. For most of the rest of Peter's life he learned from my mistakes. But that was one lesson I learned from him.

Peter and I grew up the way any normal children would. My

mother's parents lived downstairs, and I remember as a young boy that Memere and Pepere had a great big old collie, but I can't remember the dog's name. I must have enjoyed the dog as a youngster, because in my adult years I have always owned a dog.

We had a swimming pool in our backyard, and Wednesday was pool day which meant the relatives could come over for a day of swimming and relaxation. I remember setting up the pool with my Dad but I'm not sure how much help I was. I remember Dad digging up and wheel barreling the dirt over to a trailer parked in the driveway. I remember thinking I could help him by adjusting the plank that bridged the space between the trailer and the wall. As he crossed the plank with the wheelbarrow full of dirt, the plank gave way and he tumbled onto his butt and into the trailer. The bruise he received on his butt near his hip never went away. I think he wanted to choke me for helping him, but as he did throughout his whole life, he just took it in stride. We enjoyed the pool for many years to come.

I remember another time when I decided to help my Dad by backing the car out of the garage. I was a little older then. I had the strength, with the car door open, to put my foot on the cement floor and with the car in neutral, use my leg to push and get the car to roll backward. I never realized that the car would roll back so quickly, and I didn't get the car door closed quick enough before it hit the partition and came to a stop. "But I was trying to help Dad!" I shouted as he came barreling out of the house to see what had happened. Luckily, there was no damage to the car. My ego, however, was quite bruised.

I remember visits to my aunts, uncles, and cousins' homes for celebrations of all varieties. My Aunt Theresa had a piano and everyone played a "concerto." We would dance the limbo while someone played. Everyone got a turn—but the concertos were actually on the rolls of a player piano!

As Peter and I got older we would take walks up and down the street with our parents. That's when I began to meet the neighbors and their children. As we grew older, we got permission to go outside and play with the neighborhood children. It was here that I met with my first notion of being adopted. My parents never hid that fact from me; but it was the questions from the neighborhood kids that caused me to first ponder the question and what it all meant. People being people, I'm sure their parents must have spoken openly in their homes about "Peter and Paul being adopted."

Eventually, a parent's loose talk will become a child's innocent question, and they asked me, each in their own way, "So what happened to your *real* Mom and Dad?" The question may have been reasonable and even innocent to them, but it troubled me and did not have a clue how to answer. My "real" parents, I thought, were right upstairs! Knowing that I was adopted, I felt like I owed the kids some kind of answer, so I would make things up. "They were killed in a car crash" I would say, or "they died in a fire." But I had no idea of the truth. And that caused my mind to wander and question everything I thought I knew about myself.

It was one simple question, but it opened a hole that I would spend a lifetime trying to fill.

CHAPTER TWO
Learning to be Adopted

Before grammar school, I attended a private preschool. Our teacher's name was Mademoiselle Lousignant and I recall she ran a tight ship. It was 1960 so I don't really remember too many of the other details about the place. But I do know that through the years, there were other people that remembered her. Her instruction in this preschool was so good that I was considered prepared enough to skip the first grade and enter right into the second grade.

In the third grade, I remember something that I think everyone who was alive at that time remembers. The loudspeaker came on in the classroom and the announcement was made, "President Kennedy has been shot." I don't think any of us knew what that really meant, but we all knew it was bad. I remember watching the funeral procession on TV when the president's small son, John, saluted his Dad as the casket rolled by. Over the years, seeing that image always touched my heart. Certain things never leave your mind or your memory.

When I was in the fifth grade, my Mom helped me practice for a spelling bee. She seemed to think it was important that I practiced spelling what I thought was every word in the dictionary. When I questioned her, she would say, "But you never know what word they are going to ask you to spell." And so we practiced. And practiced. And practiced.

Then came the day of the big spelling bee. I took my place up on the stage and it began. I managed to get a few words spelled correctly, but I ended up stumbling and missing one. I was sad not only because I disappointed my Mom, but also because I made a mistake. As I walked back to my chair and sat next to my Mom, I cried. My Mom asked me, "Why are you crying? You did good!" I do not know why, but I think I was embarrassed.

In the sixth grade we had a female lay teacher who was not a nun. I remember she told us that she had been overseas volunteering for the Peace Corps. She seemed pretty cool. During one of her classes she explained that if someone could empty their mind of all thoughts, they would become weightless and people would be able to lift that person right off the ground without much effort at all. She asked if anyone thought that they could empty their mind that way and I volunteered. She proceeded to have me sit up on a desk in the front of the class and concentrate on thinking about nothing at all while encouraging the other kids to remain quiet. After a while I can remember that I had nothing left in my thoughts and although I seemed to be outside myself, I still had a notion of my surroundings. Students approached both sides of the desk and placed two fingers under my arms and two fingers behind my bent knees. Amazingly, they were able to life me off the desk without much effort at all, just as she said.

My next accomplishment came when I was in sixth grade and I was cast in a play where I was the lead and I had to remember all my lines. My Mom rehearsed with me until I was speaking those lines in my sleep. The play went off without a hitch. I was a one-day star!

For some reason the seventh grade was a particularly memorable year. As I was enrolled in a Catholic parochial school, this was the year I remember studying our faith. We even all attended Mass on Good Fridays. I didn't realize at the time how important those lessons would be, and how I would carry them with me throughout my entire life.

It was in the seventh and eighth grades where I also learned that kids could be cruel. Those are the years when the testosterone really kicks-in and boys really start to be boys. There were a few kids in my class who were all that—and they knew it, too. Big Gene V. and Corky G. were the class thugs, or at least I believed they were. There are a few others who seemed to want to pick on me too. And one incident with them was about to change my life.

On that day, I was walking home from school and a few of them decided they wanted to beat me up. (Who knows why.) So when I got home, I told my Mom who in turn told my Dad that a few of the boys had jumped me and beat me up. The next day my father brought me to school on his way to work and we went to see the principal. He told the principal that he wanted those kids talked to and that he did not want me being jumped anymore. My dad also proceeded to tell me that next time, I would have to defend myself in a one-on-one conflict. I was never sure how word go out so quickly that my Dad said that I was allowed to fight one-on-one if I had to, but it did. Corky was the first to come looking for me in the school yard. When I realized I had to defend myself, I wound up and punched him square in the nose. His nose bled, and mercifully I was rescued by one of the nuns almost immediately after I hit him. Thank God!

Next I remember big Gene hit me in the head with a chair in Mr. D's class, and I got up and fought him as best I could. But I was lucky that Mr. D, who seemed to me to be seven feet tall, rescued me from big Gene. A few more of these school yard scuffles and I was on my way to being left alone, thank goodness.

I learned such a valuable lesson from this. No matter how many people like my parents or teachers were there to look out for me, I learned I couldn't always rely on them. I learned I had to stand-up for myself.

During those years we used to frequent Cass Park which was just down the street from my house. During the summer there were camp counselors and different activities for the kids to do there during the day. It was a meeting place for many children. They had activities like baseball, arts and crafts, swing sets, monkey bars, and even a pond where you could go fishing, catch frogs, and get covered in mud.

In the winter there were two hockey rinks and a pond for skating. Those hockey rinks were where I learned to play hockey. Hockey would become a big winter pastime for me. We would skate all day and only go home for meals. There was always a friend at the rink and you could almost always find enough guys hanging around to start a game. I never played organized hockey, but I do wish I had. Because he grew up during the Depression, my Dad was far more concerned about me getting a good education than he was about me playing sports. He just didn't encourage me or take it seriously.

In our area, there were only a few hockey rinks. So at times, organized hockey teams would come to our rinks to practice. This is where I got the opportunity to skate with players from the Providence College hockey team. One fellow in particular named Steve took us under his wing. He taught us how to become better hockey players. He had us skate forward and backward until we could skate equally fast in both directions. He showed us the right way to handle the puck and the importance of keeping your eyes up and on the other players. We practiced passing the puck back and forth while never looking down at the ice. We became very proficient at the game.

When I looked ahead to the ninth grade, my parents arranged for me to attend Mount Saint Charles Academy, a private Catholic high school with a noted powerhouse hockey team. I was okay with the idea because I thought it would give me an opportunity to play hockey. I easily passed the entrance exam and was accepted into the school. Let me remind you that my Dad was paying for my education and he could not have cared less about me playing hockey. I, on other hand, thought high school was a waste of time. Though I know now the rigid structure they provided would come to be essential to my future career. The school did live up to its reputation as a top college preparatory school. The curriculum was tough, the Brothers who taught there were tough, and the hockey program was tough.

I remember a few instances interacting with the Brothers. Brother Girard taught the freshman English class. During one of his classes, big John P. who sat in the back row, fell asleep on his desk. As Brother Girard screamed John's name, he quickly pulled a basketball out from under his desk. As John raised his head, Brother Girard heaved the basketball with razor accuracy hitting Big John in the face knocking him off his chair and into the wall. WHAM! The shot was so accurate that you know for sure it was not the first time Brother Girard had heaved that ball. In fact, I think he practiced that shot.

Unfortunately, I would be the next recipient of a Brother's justice. It was in Brother Tardif's chemistry class where I fell asleep at my desk. Chemistry class was definitely not the most exciting thing in my life, and so I simply dozed off. I remember hearing my name screamed out loud, and as I jerked my head up off the desk, Brother Tardif slapped my face knocking me and my chair into the aisle. I was so startled that I yelled at him so he sent me to the office where I promptly got suspended. That suspension was the first of a few (more on that later). Classes were exceedingly difficult, but it was definitely a rigorous learning environment.

And then there was hockey practice. In those days, the high school recruited student hockey players from all over the country and Canada. And there I was with a ten-dollar pair of ice skates and a few bargain basement accessories. I was an unknown to the coaches since I had never played organized hockey. And because of that, it seemed as though I was in everyone's crosshairs. I was talented enough to be able to keep up with them all, and I tried my best. I did not have any support and was there on my own. And it felt that way. In the beginning, all the experienced players never even batted an eye in my direction. But there was a crazy Canadian guy named Joe G. who became my friend. But that was not until after my failed attempt to make the team. Toward the end of the tryout to make the team, I injured my ankle and was told by the doctors at the emergency room that I suffered a hairline fracture. I had to let it heal so my hockey career was placed on hold. I returned to the ice the next season only to find that I had severe ankle pain and was unable to keep up the skating pace necessary to compete. Years later I would discover that the real injury was torn ligaments.

It was in the tenth grade that I started into a phase of my life that I wish I could do over. Fair warning—there are no do overs! You only get one chance at the important things in life, so you better make those chances count.

During the tenth grade, I managed to find my way up to Chipman's Corner. Chipman's Corner was a place where kids didn't do much except hang out and get into mischief. I would be no exception. I already knew the kids from our street, so we ventured to the next street, to the next, and to the next, until we had ourselves a new band of brothers. From Rodman Street, Teddy Gabor, Stormin' Normand Gabor, myself, and Ted S. were the major characters. From Kenwood Street, Don, Ron, and Armand M. were from the same family and there were enough of them (three more brothers and two sisters) that they could have had their own gang. From Loring Street there was Ron, Bert, Guy, Billy H., Gene and Bob. And from down the street there was Ray who always hung around with Ron. From Manilla Street there was Mark L. and John E. From Olympia Avenue came the one and only Donald who I called "Frere" (French for brother). Another good friend from a little down the road was Mark D. And then there was Dennis who we called "Jap." Jap's nickname came from his combined French-Canadian and Native American background that gave him an almost Asian appearance. Crazy John W. was from East Woonsocket. Crazy John and Jap seemed to compete to be the craziest among us.

We lived at a dangerous time. The world was discovering sex, drugs, and rock and roll and we were happy to join in right along with them. It was tough keeping up with all these whackos, especially for a kid who was trying to fill an emptiness and find out who he really was. But later, it did help me understand that you are ultimately responsible for your own decisions, even if you are at times being dragged in all the wrong directions.

Hanging around at Chipman's Corner helped me get to know not only the kids who grew up around me, but those who hung out at other places around the city. There are so many more names I could list. And to this day, I still consider them all to be my friends.

CHAPTER 3
Escape

Even with all the new friends that I was making, I never felt good enough, and I found myself immersed in things that I knew were not in my best interest. As I made my way up to Chipman's Corner each day, I encountered firsthand a new wave of all the dangers crashing into the youth of our country.

First for me it was alcohol, then marijuana, and right on up the drug ladder I went. Thankfully, I did not like needles or the idea of injecting drugs. I stopped short of intravenous drug use even though I watched as many of my friends did. Oh, and I forgot to mention the LSD, mescaline, and THC. *Lions and tigers and bears! Oh my!*

While experimenting with different kinds of drugs and alcohol, I did not realize it at the time, but I was using these substances to fill the void. I felt there was something missing, that somehow, I wasn't complete. I could never be as good as all my friends and the alcohol and drugs helped—or so I thought. In truth, it made it worse. I don't admit this now to make you feel sorry for me, that's not the point. The reason is to stop other kids from doing this. It doesn't work, it's dangerous, and can lead to so many worse things. Don't do it.

After finishing the tenth grade and realizing that I would

never have a hockey career, I transferred to public school at Woonsocket High School. Luckily for me, the curriculum at Mount St. Charles Academy was much more advanced than the public school curriculum, and I was able to breeze through two years at Woonsocket High without having to study at all.

Just like in elementary school, there were incidents in high school that will always stay etched in my memory. As I transferred to a new school, I remained thankful for the friends I had made at Chipman's Corner. Those friends made the transition much easier. For a time, I became the manager for the hockey team which meant that I was to keep track of the equipment and things of that nature. Coming from Mount, and having skated (to a degree) there, I was asked to play hockey for the Woonsocket team. But I knew that I couldn't due to the pain I felt in my ankle when I skated.

Life at Woonsocket High School was somewhat of a gray time for me. I was a friendly person, and so I was able to easily make many new friends in this new school. However, I had been bitten by the drug bug which was an unfortunate occurrence in my life. Let me say here and now that all types of drugs are bad. There are those people who would try to tell you otherwise, but I say they are fools. Our culture seems to be headed down a slippery slope with several states in the process of legalizing marijuana. If you try hard enough, I guess you can convince anyone of just about anything. But I digress…

As I started to say, life at Woonsocket High School, as I reflect for this story, was a gray time. Because of my drug use I did not retain the memories of academics that I should have. I remember the faces and some of the names, but the things I was in school to learn, I did not remember. I would also add that drug use robbed me of my incentive and direction in addition to my memory. When I should have been focusing on my future and direction in life, instead all I could think about was getting and staying high.

I remember seeing my friends during the time between classes, and we would goof on how high we were. As I think back on that, it brings a tear to my eyes. Not just for me but for every kid that has ever or will ever get caught up in drug use and experience the same thing.

As my high school years wound down, I started to realize that I did not have any life direction in mind of any kind. Years of scanning and searching faces in the crowd, not even sure who I was looking for, made life feel surreal. How can you be sure about what direction to take when don't know who you are? I think I was concerned about all that, but the drugs were a heavy mask. As I mentioned before, some things stay with you.

On graduation day, my mom, dad, and grandmother were so proud and wanted me to go with them to a celebration dinner. But instead I went to a small bar around the corner with one of my friends for their 25-cent draft beers. We each drank 42 glasses of beer that night. I am not sure why I remember that. I believe that God has a way of sticking our mistakes deep inside our brains so that we never forget them.

The other thing that wore heavily on my mind was the hormonal drive to find a girlfriend. During my latter years of high school, hot pants became the new fad. The awkwardness of newfound sexuality also made life increasingly more difficult. Those pressures did nothing except increase my need to fill the void.

So here came the girls. I fell for a girl in high school who pranced around in hot pants and tortured me with her good-natured flirting. But she had her sights set on one of the boys in the band. It would be about five years until we met up again.

Then I met Jodi. She was the most beautiful girl that I had ever seen. I was 18 and she was only 15. She was a pretty girl with bright eyes and a bright smile. She was so easy to be around. Whenever we walked somewhere together, to this day I do not remember my feet touching the ground. She was my first true love.

But she was also Daddy's little girl, and Daddy was no fan of me. One fateful day three months after Jodi and I met, Daddy stood waiting in the back yard with shotgun in hand, to make sure I got the message to stay away. I was absolutely crushed. If she reads this book, she's going to find out right now that I spent three nights in a sleeping bag in the field behind her house just to be near her. And on and on it went. That void I felt remains very hard to explain to this day. We all feed the beast in a different way I suppose. I guessed that if drugs and alcohol weren't filling that void, maybe love and sex would.

CHAPTER 4

"God doesn't take away the time you spend fishing…"

Starting in my youth, fishing at Cass Park in Woonsocket grew into a great love of being on the water and fishing. Every opening day in Rhode Island we would prepare for some trout fishing at Cass Park. The State of Rhode Island has always done a great job raising fish and stocking ponds across the state with several different species of trout.

As my friends and I grew older, we ventured out to several different ponds in our area. There would be a lot to learn about fishing as we would find out on every trip—live bait versus lures, light test lines versus heavier lines, light whippy rods… Little did I know that it would take years to figure it all out. So many ponds and streams and so little time!

As life went on, fishing became a way to empty my head. It was an opportunity to sort things out in my mind without interference from the clutter of constant chit-chat. In a way, it did fill that void, if only temporarily.

My first big fish came in my late teens on Sneech Pond fishing with live shiners from the bank. I had caught a few smaller fish, but when this one hit and I set the hook, I knew it was going to be a huge bass! After I reeled it in, I took it to a local bait store and the fish was measured and weighed. She was a 22-inch long, six-pound beauty of a large mouth bass. I left it there to be mounted and set out to tell everyone about my very first big bass fish story! As fate would have it that would be the last time I ever saw that fish again.

I had saved the money I needed to pay for the mounting, but when I went back to the shop to pay the bill, the small building was empty. I was frantic and hurried up to the house. I banged on the first-floor door and inquired of the lady, "What happened to the shop and where was my big bass?" She apologized and said that her husband had died and her relatives had cleaned out the shop. She was sorry but she had no idea what happened to the fish. I wanted to be angry, but how could I be? The woman had lost her husband after all.

I believe that my first boat came along when I was about 20 years old. I had an old Chevy pickup and purchased a 12-foot fiberglass Sears Game Fisher with a 7 ½ horsepower Game Fisher outboard motor. I purchased a new trailer for the boat, too, and we were off—from one pond to the next.

At the time I lived in Woonsocket, but there was a pond in the southern part of the state that was over an hour away called Worden's Pond. The pond held a good population of bass, but it was also known for its good northern pike population, too. I was heading there with my pal Dupes one morning when along the way we stopped to check on the live bait. We had 'O' tabs with us to drop in the water to give more oxygen to the fish. I pried the tightly fit cover off the 'O' tabs can, but in the process I sliced my finger open. Dupes said, "Hey, we gotta get you to the emergency room for stitches!" But I declined. "We are going fishing," I insisted as I wrapped my finger with napkins and duct tape. We fished for hours. I still have a small scar to remind me of that day.

On another trip to Worden's Pond with my old buddy Skip, I

learned a valuable lesson about rod strength. For this trip we prepared for some pike fishing by catching some golden shiners for bait near the dam at Stillwater Reservoir. Then we headed out for a day on the water. We hooked up with steel leaders to prevent line breakage from the fish's teeth and slowly trolled about the lake. A few bites here and there, but that big one eluded us… until we watched in awe as a giant pike broke a wake across the surface and headed directly for my bait. The wake had to be five to six inches wide at the front which meant a huge pike was about to swallow my shiner!

As the huge pike grabbed hold of his meal, I opened the bale. Pike tend to grab at bait sideways and chomp on it as they turn it to swallow it. He was emptying the bale while swimming away, so I had to make a move! Slowly I closed the bale so as not to alert the giant. As the line became taught, I set the hook. With a whippy-tipped rod I never got a good hookset, and after a quick twist of the giant's head, I watched him swim away. The rod never saw the light of day again. Another fishing lesson learned!

I have been a very lucky guy when it comes to fishing for largemouth bass. My cousin Tom lives in Florida and loves fishing. He has taken me out on many a lake in Florida. The greatest trip by far was to Lake Weohyakapka (the name is Indian and means *walk in the water*). We set out on that first morning with great anticipation.

With a live well full of healthy wild shiners, we set up near a group of tall reeds and tossed out our lines. Within a minute it was on! A huge bass pushed my shiner to the surface, swirled around it, and down it went. As I set the hook, I knew it was a giant. I had never felt a bass pull so hard. What a fight she put up (the larger bass are usually female). Cousin Tom's 20-foot ranger boat spun round and round. Finally, she tired herself out and was netted. It turned out to be a 9.25-pound giant. My biggest bass ever!

We caught a few smaller bass and decided to move the boat up to a point on the reed line. Anchors down, we tossed our bait into the water, and it wasn't long before I had another giant bass on the end! After another awesome battle, my cousin and I boated my second huge bass—this one weighed in at 10.25 pounds! After logging thousands of hours on the water, I caught the two biggest bass of my life in under one hour!

I had read that during the wintertime in Florida the hydrilla weeds would die off up to three or four feet below the water line. While drifting a live shiner 10 feet off the bobber, the bait would swim slowly over the hydrilla and the bass would shoot up from the weeds and slam the bait.

We caught a few bluebird days where the wind gently pushed the boat across the lake, and this was the perfect time to test this new technique. We did exactly as I had read, and we got down to some very relaxing fishing. But we wouldn't be relaxing for long. The technique worked incredibly well with bass coming one after the other. We caught several bass in the 5, 6, 7, and 8-pound class! It was and still remains the best few days of largemouth bass fishing my cousin and I ever enjoyed! Over the years, Cuz took us out on Rodman Reservoir, St. John's River, Istopoga, Kissimmee, Apopka, The Harris Chain, and Okeechobee, to name a few.

When you log as many hours as I have fishing for largemouth bass, you learn a few things—and I have.

I have also been very lucky to have had a great ocean fishing teacher, Dean (Leroy) Ingalls, my former father-in-law. Leroy was an old salt who knew ocean fishing extremely well. We used to go out near the power plant next to Battleship Cove in Massachusetts quite often. The warm water coming out of the plant and flowing into the cove brought in many unusual species of fish, and fishing there was always very good.

I remember being out there one day with Leroy near the power plant when we saw a fish that looked like a shark's fin move fairly close to the boat. Keep in mind that the boat was just a fiberglass twelve-footer with a 9.5 horsepower Evinrude outboard motor, so when I saw it, I was quick to say, "Let's get out of here." Leroy laughed out loud saying, "Really kid? It's just a giant sunfish!" We idled the boat closer, and after shutting off the engine we were able to get very close to it. It was huge and beautiful and a sight to behold!

And now one last story about fishing…

A group of friends and I decided to charter a boat for an ocean fishing trip. We set out from the Port of Galilee in Rhode Island for a day of striper fishing. We were having a ball catching stripers in the waters off Block Island. If I remember correctly, we may have even caught a few small tuna!

Our captain who was up in the fly bridge said he could see something odd happening off in the distance. He explained that a lobster pot buoy kept going under water and popping back up. The captain motored us over to the area and it wasn't long before we all realized what was happening. A giant sea turtle had become tangled in a lobster pot line! As the boat approached, the giant turtle tried to swim away pulling the buoy under as it struggled. The captain pulled back while he and the mate could decide on a plan. Keep in mind that these giant turtles can grow up to 7 feet and weigh 2,000 pounds.

The captain backed the boat slowly towards the buoy, and the mate used a long pole to grab the lobster pot line. The turtle took off and we were all very surprised at the strength of the animal as it pulled a 38-foot boat loaded to the gills. After an hour of pulling and tugging by five grown men, we finally pulled her up to the side of boat. Now the untangling of the lobster pot could begin. Somehow the turtle was not convinced that we were trying to help her, and she struggled to pull away while four men hung on tight and two other men cut at the line with very sharp knives. The line was wrapped tightly around the giant turtle's front legs and neck. In fact, the rope had even become partially wedged under her shell.

It was a painstaking process—pull the turtle back to the boat and cut away at the rope, then the big turtle would swim away, and we would pull her back to the boat again for more cutting. Finally only one cut remained. My hands were on the rope closest to the turtle's neck as my friend reached down to make the last cut. No more than a foot separated my hands from the turtle, and I said to my friend, "Steady hands, eh?" He gave me a reassuring nod.

I want to add at this point just how huge this giant really was. Her eyeball was the size of a grapefruit and her shell was as big as the top of a Volkswagen! She also exhibited incredible swimming strength, being able to swim away from the boat repeatedly all while four grown men hung on tight!

And with one last cut she was free!

Fishing has, and always will, offer me a great reprieve and escape from the stresses of life.

CHAPTER 5
The Farm

The first year or two after high school I did not know what to do with myself. I was doing a good job of maintaining my degree in sex, drugs and rock 'n roll, but not much else. I floated from job to job but was unable to find my niche. Many of the jobs were menial at best, and I was too much of a scatter-brain to remain interested in anything for too long.

Meanwhile, I filled my time and the void in my life by continuing to experiment with drugs and with women. It seems that in my life I have had quite a few girlfriends—so many, in fact, that I am a bit embarrassed by it. But not having much to offer any woman, relationships were difficult to maintain and didn't last long. Looking back, each girl that I met brought with them their own special "something" but looking everywhere (except right under my nose), I failed to see anything except what I needed and wanted. I was so wrapped up in looking that I never really appreciated what I had already found.

All the useful things that I learned from my faith-based Catholic education had vanished from my thoughts. Right and wrong were mixed up and lost in a thick fog. I walked blindly forward and stumbled into many pitfalls.

Nightly, I would make my way up to Chipman's Corner to

hang out with my friends. There was a liquor store at the bottom of the street—Bert's Liquors—where just about anyone could buy alcohol. I was not of age at the time, but it seemed that all you needed was a beard and they didn't ask questions. I remember taking liquor orders from my friends—a bottle of this, a pint of that, a GIQ of beer—you name it. Then we would head up into the woods behind Chipman's Corner to make huge bonfires, sit, drink, smoke weed, and do whatever drugs anyone had brought along.

Hallucinogenic drugs were a bit of a rage during those years. Mescaline was a milder hallucinogenic drug that was popular at the time. I can remember tripping on sunny days with my friends and chasing rainbow trout through the stream that flowed through the woods. The woods always seemed to take on more intensity while on drugs. At that moment it seemed to be the coolest thing anyone could do, but in truth, it was just the continuation of a stupid waste of time. I learned there is no future in drugs.

I witnessed many things that were absolutely scary. Some of my friends were using intravenous drugs. Whatever was available in pill form, these guys would cook up and then shoot up. I watched friends eyes roll up and pass out after shooting up. Later these guys would come to and say how great they felt. "Yah right," I would say. I can't tell you how many times those friends said, "Come on, Paul, try it." I thank God I never did.

I remember one of our gang liked to use heroin. He often convinced us that he could buy us a very good bag of weed, but when we pitched in and gave him the money, he would head straight to his dealer to buy heroin. Then we would not see him for days as he holed-up alone to do his drugs. I am not sure why we never gave him a beating for stealing from us, but we never did. Years later his drug use would kill him.

Drug and alcohol use among my friends would continue to wreak havoc with all our lives then and through the years. One friend continued to abuse and died when he was about 45 years old. Another friend who continued to abuse just plain disappeared and hasn't been heard from again. And still another who was caught dealing drugs left this area and moved to California. He became a bounty hunter (sounds exciting) but ended up being killed when someone he had helped arrest got out of jail and exacted his revenge. He shot my friend while he lay sleeping.

John, Mich, Russell, and T—all gone because of drugs. And my friend, Jap, just disappeared. When my cousin was a practicing attorney in California, she tried to help me find Jap but to no avail. I think of all of them from time to time wondering what life would be like if they were still here. Just recently I heard a rumor that Jap's dead body was found on the side of a jogging path somewhere in California. I was told he died of a gunshot wound, but I don't think I will ever know for sure. There was no record of the death that I could find so I wonder if he could still be alive. Jail maybe?

Especially painful was the loss of my good friend Frere. He committed suicide. I was crushed. Frere was a scrapper, and he and I had what my friends would call the best fight ever. No one thought he could be beat until the night that he and I would have at it.

One of my buddy's parents happened to be on vacation and we had the run of his house. (Of course, alcohol and drugs were involved.) Before you knew it, Frere and I were arguing about something, and not too long after that, we ended up in a fight. The next day when everyone arrived at Chipman's Corner, word spread that Maintz (my nickname) and Frere had fought. People quickly assumed Frere must have won. But those who witnessed the fight shook their heads and said no, Maintz won! Frere and

I showed up at the corner soon thereafter and it was plain to see by just looking at Frere that he had gotten the worst of it. Bobby V, one of the older guys in the group, made me and Frere shake hands—and that was that. I may have gotten the best of him, but I did not feel like a winner. We were best buddies. I felt like shit.

Frere was a wanderer. Without warning, he would often just take off for parts unknown. One time he ended up in the Grand Canyon with another friend of ours. And another time he ended up in Independence, California living with some self-proclaimed "guru." I remember when he returned from that trip. I met up with him one night and he was eager to tell me all about it. I will never forget one thing he said. The guru told me, "When you are too old to learn, then you are ready to die." Like I said before, some things just stick with you.

Frere's suicide took place sometime when I was in my late 20's. I was married at that point, had a child, and I was working hard to make ends meet. Frere came to my house one day—he just showed up looking skinny and frail wearing multiple layers of clothing saying he was trying to stay warm. He begged me to let him sleep in my basement and then take him to work with me, but I just couldn't do it. I had a job, a kid, responsibilities… and I didn't want to get dragged back into that scene myself. If memory serves me correctly, it was the last time I saw him alive.

Frere's suicide devastated me. I carried a lot of guilt about that day for a very long time because he asked for my help and I was unable to do what he needed. Frere's mom said there would be no funeral because she couldn't afford one. I called the funeral home to request that I be allowed to see my friend before he was buried. The director said that I would need his Mom's permission and she gave it without hesitation.

It was a large room on the first floor of the funeral home and my friend was lying on a stainless-steel table covered only with a sheet. The funeral home director stood in the doorway as I approached the table. Frere looked very white and cold and I wished for a moment that he had a blanket to keep him warm. Looking back, I remember being incredibly guilty and sad, but also angry with him. I took a deep breath and then I slapped him hard in the face and told him to get up and fight. "You had no right to do this!" I yelled at him. Crying, I walked away. Rest in peace, Frere.

I think it was the summer of 1995 when my friend Mark L. was visiting me from his home in Colorado. During the conversation, Frere's name came up and it was then that Mark told me of Frere's struggle with bipolar disorder. Mark said that Frere refused to take the lithium drug that was prescribed to him because it made him feel weird. I was stunned. I had always worried that Frere went to hell because he killed himself, but now I had reason to hope that because he was not in his right mind he was safely in heaven. Like I said before, some things just stick with you.

Bringing the story back more into focus, it's important that I speak about me continuing to try to fill that void. There was one thing that did make a difference.

I was in my late teens when I was introduced to the construction trades. Thank goodness, because it was in the trades where I found my niche. Carpentry and construction afforded me the opportunity to learn many things, and I enjoyed doing them. Little did I know then that in a few short years I would be striking out on my own. I set my sights to gain knowledge of the roofing and siding trades. Seeing many people muddle along as laborers year after year I knew that I could be better than that—but I had to rise to the top. So I decided to apprentice with some good teachers and I tried to learn quickly.

I was on a job site one day when the owner of the company

left me alone with a helper and said, "This is an easy wall and you should have no trouble completing it." He was right—and I did complete it. Then I realized one wall was just like the next, and there wasn't any wall I couldn't handle. At the next opportunity, I spoke with the boss and voiced my wishes. "From now on I would like to be paid on the books so that I can collect in the winter when it's too cold to work. I would also like a raise in wages because you now know you can count on me to run a wall." He flatly refused and I walked away.

At the time I was living on "The Farm" with the girl who was to become my first wife. Remember that girl in high school with the hot pants that wanted the band guy instead of me? The Farm was part of a spectacular 100-acre parcel of land in the northern part of Rhode Island that bordered a reservoir, which was surrounded by another 1,000 acre natural watershed. We lived on the first floor of an old farmhouse that was heated only by firewood. Upstairs lived Joe and Julie who would become lifelong dear friends. Joe and I were in our early 20's and the two of us were about to start out as our own bosses.

I would like to tell you a bit of how we came to live at the farm. I had answered a classified ad that read, *House to share with the right couple. Please call…* I was curious, so I called. Joe answered the phone and said that we could come to see the place right away. We drove out to this farmhouse that overlooked a beautiful reservoir at the end of a long dirt driveway. "Wow" was all that I could say as we came upon the place.

Julie was at work, so Joe gave us a tour of the place. The central living room was on the first floor, and there was a large Shenandoah woodstove piped to the chimney. "That's the heating system!" Joe said watching me for my reaction. But this place was much too beautiful for me to be dissuaded by something so simple, so I asked, "Where do we get the firewood?"

Joe answered quickly. "We cut it from the woods around the property. In fact, I was about to go out and cut right now."

I looked at my girl and said, "Leave me here to cut wood with Joe and I will call you to come and get me when we are done." She did as I asked and Joe and I went off together. I'm sure Joe had to be wondering to himself about going out to cut wood with me when he had not even talked with Julie yet about us living there. We filled his truck with wood, came back to the house, and stacked the wood on the porch. My girlfriend had come back to pick me up, and Joe and I shook hands. He said he would call us.

He called later that night and said we could have the room on the first floor. We were ecstatic and proceeded to move in right away. Living at The Farm was amazing. Joe, Julie, and I are still best of friends to this day. In fact, I am proud to be the godfather of their oldest daughter.

That farmhouse was the easiest living that I would ever enjoy. It was a time in my life that I remember with great fondness. Friends would come by and we would head down to the water to fish or to swim or to just sit and get high and enjoy the beauty of nature around us. But through it all, the nagging feeling of my own lost identity haunted me. No matter how good things were, the void was still there. It wouldn't go away.

While we were living on The Farm, Joe and Julie were building a house in Jackson, Maine. It wouldn't be too long before they would be moving on. They both had become my dear friends and I am thankful to be their friend to this day.

The old saying, "a reason, a season, or a lifetime" is appropriate. They are lifetime friends.

Farm living continued to be good for a few years, and I would eventually marry my first wife while living on The Farm. As things would have it though, the rug was about to be pulled out from under our feet. We had planned to have our wedding there. Two weeks before the wedding, the new owner of The Farm, knowing full well that our wedding was coming soon, decided to plow up all the fields and turn those majestic rolling hay fields into fields of dirt and mud. I was furious with the new owner but there was nothing I could do. We had no choice but to go on with the wedding on The Farm anyway.

CHAPTER 6
Visions

My connection with Native American tradition began with a simple trip down a local highway. As I drove along, up ahead, I could see another vehicle. Suddenly the car's brake lights came on, and I was curious as to why because there were no other vehicles anywhere near it. As my car approached the area where the driver had hit the brakes, I saw a very large red-tailed hawk lying on the ground off to the side of the road. I pulled off the road and stopped the car on the shoulder. I rushed over to that beautiful bird, and when I picked it up, I realized that it was still alive.

What I saw next would have a profound effect on the rest of my life. I held that beautiful bird carefully in my hands. It reached up at me with those big powerful feet and talons, and his look as our eyes met seemed to cut right through me. It was a look that I will never forget. Later on in my life, Eagle Bear, a Native American friend who I came to know years later, would say that when the hawk died in my hands, it left me with his spirit.

My affinity for birds of prey had started much earlier in life, when I was just a kid. My Dad had been in the Navy during World War II. During a stopover in Italy, he purchased a statue of a falcon and bookends of eagle heads all cut from granite which I proudly still display on my mantle. I remember learning in grade school about the falcon and the eagle which increased my respect for these wonderful creatures even more. They are majestic birds with their own individual attributes needed for their survival.

Also, my friend Jap, as I mentioned, was of Native American heritage. One day his father told us the story of the hawk. He told us that whenever a Native American would set out on a journey, whether it be hunting, fishing, or searching out a camp site, to see a hawk fly overhead meant that the journey will be protected by the spirit of the hawk. From then on, anytime I went on a journey and saw a hawk fly over, I knew that my trip would be protected by that hawk's spirit.

Over the years I discovered another curious fact. It would also seem that if I happened to be speaking about a particular topic and a hawk flew overhead while I was speaking, whatever I was saying would turn out to be true.

After that hawk died in my hands, I took it home and carefully wrapped in many layers of paper and placed it in the freezer to preserve it. Initially I thought I might find someone to mount this beautiful bird of prey for me but I soon realized that because of this birds protected status, no one would touch it.

Being unable to find a taxidermist that would mount the hawk, I had to look somewhere else. I was aware of a Native American powwow being held in a neighboring town, so I made it a point to attend. Upon arriving, I came upon a large circle, and at the center of the circle was a campfire. Later I would come to learn that this was a fire circle. A fire circle was a place of great reverence, as the fire represented life.

I had been told to seek out a medicine man named Little Turtle and that he would guide me regarding what to do with the hawk. It turned out the gentleman had grown old and as such directed me to a man they called Eagle Bear. I was able to find a woman named Loving One who helped put me in touch with Eagle Bear.

Eagle Bear took his knowledge of Native American tradition very seriously. He explained to me that in the old days, a Native American would never share his knowledge of medicine, or of healing, with any white man. This sentiment of resentment had come from the treatment of the Native American people. Knowing the history of our country, I could understand this sentiment. He informed me that his teacher had said to "enlighten those who seek out the knowledge" so our friendship was forged. Over the next 20 years, I would benefit greatly from his knowledge of Native American tradition. I remember Eagle Bear took his time showing me the way. As with any traditional knowledge, learning is a process. (My studies of Okinawan karate have taught me that.)

Eagle Bear and I became the best of friends. He taught me much about Native American tradition. The importance of the fire, the lessons to be learned from the wildlife, and the knowledge of plants that can be used for food and medicine. We shared our stories about each other's lives as friends would. We gained much knowledge of each other's trials and triumphs on our way through this life. The things that I learned from Native American teachings would prove to be very valuable to future realizations.

My most vivid recollections from these experiences were of the spirit fire and the sweat lodge. But before I elaborate on those thoughts, I would like to share something that Eagle Bear did for my children. The kids at the time were between the ages of six and twelve years old. I remember asking them if they would like him to come and talk with them about Native American traditions. They were all very excited about it. I will never forget that Saturday afternoon. Everyone sat down on the living room floor and Eagle Bear proceeded to share his stories with them. I remember how amazed I was to see the children sit for hours and listen attentively to his words. Again, some things just stick with you.

My daughter, Amanda, had a class in high school where they built a replica Native American site in a wooded area near the school. At Amanda's request, Eagle Bear came to her school to talk to her class about Native American traditions. He made sure to tell the class that he was only there because Amanda had asked him to come.

Eagle Bear suggested that it would be good if he and I built a sweat lodge together. So one day we worked cutting maple saplings along the edge of his property. The saplings were about one inch thick and 15 or so feet in length.

After gathering the needed wood, we proceeded to use a bar about the width of the saplings to bang holes into the ground. One end of the sapling was stuck into the ground and then bent over and stuck into the ground on the opposite side. After the saplings were placed, twine was used to secure the intersections of the wood. The width of the circle of the lodge was approximately 10 feet and the height was about three and a half feet. In the center of the lodge was a hole dug in the ground that would accommodate the grandmother and grandfather stones. The lodge took some time to build, so the ceremony would have to come another day.

On the day of my first sweat lodge ceremony, there was much to be done. I was told in preparation for this day to come to the ceremony with a clear and open mind. Eagle Bear said, "Leave negative thoughts aside that you might hear or see the message from the other side." I had no idea what that really meant, or what was to come, but I took his advice and came ready for the experience.

When I arrived, Eagle Bear conducted a smudge ceremony where sage is placed on to an oyster shell and burned. I turned my body as the smoke was allowed to rise all around to purify and take away evil spirits and evil thoughts.

Next it was necessary to build the spirit fire. At the very base of this fire there were stones approximately the size of one's skull placed carefully next to each other. These stones represented all the grandmothers and grandfathers who had passed before us. During a round in the lodge, there are generally four to seven of these stones that will be used. There could be as many as 28 stones in the base of the fire.

Wood was then stacked carefully upon the stones to create a large fire. Once the fire was lit, it was important to make sure that the stones were always covered by fire. During the time the stones were being heated, tobacco was placed on the fire as an offering to the spirit world. The smell of the tobacco smoke reaching into the heavens was used to, hopefully, get the attention of the spirits of grandmothers and grandfathers on the other side. One would take a handful of tobacco and squeeze it into the palm of their hand while contemplating their request for help. Then one would place the tobacco slowly on a log at the edge of the fire to give the tobacco an opportunity to burn slowly while the smoke rises to the heavens.

The time when the fire burns and the stones are heated is a time of quiet meditation. There is usually one person assigned to be the fire keeper. This person will keep the wood fire covering the stones while lodge takes place. The fire keeper will also be responsible for bringing in the stones during the lodge ceremony. While the fire burned, it would also be the time to cover the lodge with heavy blankets so that no light would penetrate inside. These blankets were carefully laid over the frame of the lodge overlapping at every edge and doubling up over the entire structure. As this process was completed, one would continually check from inside the lodge to see if there was any light penetrating. The process was complete only when no light could be seen.

As the fire burned down and the stones became red hot, it was time for the ceremony of lodge to begin. The doorway was only big enough to allow one person to crawl through. As one crawled into the lodge, grandmother and grandfather were recognized. One would crawl through the lodge in a circular, clockwise motion taking the next available place to sit. One would sit cross legged. I should add that women went into the lodge with a loose blouse and skirt or loose dress and men went wearing only shorts.

The lodge keeper, in this case Eagle Bear, would sit in lodge opposite to the entrance. Once everyone was seated, the fire keeper with a long-pronged rake would dig stones from the fire and place them one at a time in the dugout at the center of lodge. Once the desired number of stones were placed, the door was closed and lodge would begin.

This would be a good time to remind the reader of the necessity of being in the moment, of being centered in one's self in order to be able draw the most from the ceremony of lodge.

The lodge keeper, Eagle Bear, then began the ceremony. Sweet grass was laid upon the hot stones with the sweet smell offering an invitation to grandmother and grandfather to bring their wisdom and teaching to the ceremony. Eagle Bear drummed and chanted Native American songs—another invitation to grandmother and grandfather to bring wisdom to the lodge. The people in the lodge also chanted as this was thought to be pleasing to the relations.

My first experiences with lodge were very humbling and a great learning experience. I was taught the humility of my anger and recognized my lack of control. At the time of my experience with lodge, my life was in turmoil and so lodge made sure that I understood that. At this point in my life, everything was unsettled. My marriage was heading to divorce and there was intense animosity in the relationship. The unique pressures of working with my special needs child only added to my stress and anger. And, of course, I had never come to terms with my own identity or filled that void in my life, wondering who I truly was.

I am going to recount the individual events or things that took place in my lodge ceremonies. These lessons helped me greatly with my healing.

Once the stones have been brought into the lodge and the chanting and drumming was finished, the next part of the ceremony began.

There was one other item that was brought into lodge that I have not yet mentioned. It was a container of water with a bunch of cedar bush branches tied together to form a brush of sorts. I was taught while we prepared for lodge that after a heavy rain the branches of the cedar bush or shrub, because of the density of the leaves, would hold water long after the rain had stopped. If one was thirsty and knew of this fact, they would have a drink available to them.

The drumming and chanting stopped, and the lodge keeper grabbed the cedar brush and sprinkled water onto the hot stones while continuing to chant. The resulting steam that rolled off the stones and filled the lodge seemed hot enough to boil a lobster! If people in lodge were not centered within themselves, the resulting heat would be unbearable. The lodge keeper would repeat the sprinkling of water onto the hot stones several times increasing the steam heat throughout the ceremony. After what seemed like an eternity, the lodge keeper would say loudly "open door" and the fire keeper would do so. The participants would come filing out, completely spent.

The first two times I participated in the ceremony of lodge were by far the most difficult. As much as I thought that I was in control, lodge taught me that I was not. I remember feeling totally unable to withstand the rigors of the lodge ceremony. When ceremony was over, I could not even think about going back in. This would take some getting used to and better preparation of my mind. That's what I would think about until the next ceremony.

One of the goals of the ceremony of lodge was to learn about yourself. The contemplation of the individual ceremony was the key to understanding what the message was. I would learn many things about myself in these ceremonies. For example, I learned in lodge how to handle people who are disloyal. And I learned patience.

The next ceremony that I was fortunate enough to be involved in took place at the Eagle Bear's new home and lodge site. He had prepared an area on the back of his property that was very well-suited for a ceremonial site. He planted shrubs in a circle around a fire area and lodge area. Eagle Bear's father was Native American, as was a brother, and they had lived in the house before Eagle Bear and his wife moved in. There was a good aura to the place.

Each time, the lodge ceremony was very spiritual and a time of great contemplation. The time we used to gather stone and build a fire to cover the stones was very important to me. The camaraderie that Eagle Bear and I shared are times I will never forget.

On the next occasion of lodge, as we gathered inside, I remember it being too warm and I didn't think I could handle it. Eagle Bear suggested that Mother Earth would provide me with a cool breath. He said to place my hands on the ground in a cupping motion and put my face into my hands and breathe in. As I did so I received a cool clear breath and that helped me immensely. I remember as I looked up from the ground to the roof of the lodge it seemed to glow almost a blood-red color. The weave of the blankets and the branches of the frame of the lodge seemed to me to look like veins of a sort. However, I was unable then to understand what I had just seen. I still get goosebumps just thinking about that moment.

As we came out of the lodge, I saw that it had snowed, and I recall falling face first into the ice cold snow. It felt so good I didn't want to move. After a few minutes, Eagle Bear suggested we get up out of the snow lest we get frostbite.

These things that I tell you about understanding the message of lodge were, for me, the keys to understanding the meaning of my own life from the very beginning. You see, after much contemplation, I realized that in that lodge, Creator and the spirits had taken me back to the very beginning—back to the womb! I was taken back to my very inception, from the beginning of my being which I must understand from the beginning. The lodge brought me back to this moment so that I could reevaluate my own life in the present. It showed me a path so I could start over.

When the time came for another ceremony, we repeated the acts of gathering the stones, building the fire, and enjoying the peace and serenity of the moments before lodge. Then we went inside once again. Sweet grass, the drumming, the chanting— and each time I experienced this, I grew stronger and more aware.

In this new lodge, I had the vision of a set of eyes that would come toward me and then back away. After the ceremony, Eagle Bear asked what I had seen. I said that I didn't understand right away. He told me to contemplate this vision and to ask the Creator for clarification.

I meditated on this vision for many months. And then one day, while thinking about my life before I was adopted, I realized that many times during the day a caretaker at the orphanage where I was for the first few months of my life would come to see me. She would feed me, change me, or provide care for whatever need I had, then lay me back down. Then the eyes would go away. I realized that this was the vision I experienced in the lodge.

I have heard of studies that suggest that it is very good for a newborn to be held often in the first few months of life. Writing this, I have a tear in my eye knowing that all I wanted was to be held. I didn't want those eyes to go away.

While my friendship with Eagle Bear is not what it once was, I will always love the man and have a great fondness for the Native American teachings he shared with me. *Aho*.

CHAPTER 7
Confidence through Strength

My studies of Okinawan Karate began in my early twenties with a man who would turn out to become a very dear friend—George A. It was a good many years ago, and I don't remember exactly how it came to pass, but one day George ended up at a little house I owned in Woonsocket, Rhode Island where we talked for a while. He was an active martial artist and something he sensed in me must have suggested to him that I would enjoy this study.

Little did I realize what a giant impact martial arts training would have on my life. The physical part is obvious, but the psychological impact I experienced as I progressed was the ultimate payoff. Learning how to properly defend yourself places a great restraint on a person. You realize and respect that there are consequences to all actions.

As we spoke, George enlightened me about his training. He walked over to the side of my house and picked up a red chimney brick. He knelt on the grass in my front yard with the red brick laying across his open palm. In the blink of an eye, he raised his hand then split that brick in half. I was hooked. I began training immediately.

George had been a student at the Okinawan Temple karate

studio operated by Sensei Al Gagne. He had attained the Nidan (second degree) black belt. I could tell while working with George that he thoroughly enjoyed his martial arts training. Before too long we had collected together a small group of dedicated people learning Okinawan karate together.

From the beginning, George explained that although he could give us rank, we would never be in the true circles of his instructor. For reasons which I still have no knowledge, George preferred not to continue training under Sensei Al. As such, Sensei Al would never condone our rank as George's students. We all agreed to continue our training under George, as this was what we knew. George trained us fully, as he had been trained by Sensei Al, which I believe showed his ultimate respect for the style and the system. Our training continued for a few years and then situations changed. George and his wife and family moved to Florida, and we found ourselves on our own.

Eventually, most of us contacted Sensei Al and we became his students. While he would not recognize and acknowledge our rank because George did not train under him while teaching us, we were well schooled and therefore gained our rank back quickly. The training at the Okinawan Temple was fair but very tough. This was "full contact" martial arts training. Bruises were commonplace as we conditioned our arms and legs to take the hit.

Greenbelt was the coming-of-age rank in our martial arts training—where boys turned to men I guess you could say. Reaching the rank of green belt means that the black belts and brown belts were free to use head contact while sparring. And the intensity of the training increased.

Training and sparring as a white belt and a blue belt allowed a student the luxury of head gear and a chest protector, but with a green belt those luxuries went away. No more chest protector and no more head gear—block or be hit. This was what lower rank training had been preparing us for. Conditioning of the arms and legs, continual training of blocks, punches, and kicks, and the practice of *kata* (perfecting movement) was very vigorous. I can say with total honesty that I have performed blocking, punching, and kicking drills many thousands of times and believe I can do these drills in my sleep.

A student is always a student. However, as one increases in rank, more is expected. As I was training for my brown belt, I became involved in the teaching of beginner students. Being rewarded with the opportunity to teach is a gift unto itself. The reinforcement of one's knowledge by teaching further enhances one's ability. It was important to teach in the manner that we were taught, thus continuing the tradition of our training.

The level of training at the Okinawan Temple was incredible. The groundwork, in a system that dates back several hundred years, had been laid to perfection. Matsumura Sokon, Matsumura Nabe, Sokon Hohan, Coffman James, Sensei Al Gagne, and my brother, black belts were an absolute gift.

As I stated earlier, as one continued through the ranks the training became more demanding. Brown belt was preparation for black belt, and much was expected. Working with a partner blasting punches and kicks and blocking those punches and kicks created such a mutual respect that should I never see my brothers again, I will always love and respect them. We are modern-day warriors preparing for hopefully what would always be avoided. But always ready, as we never know what is to come.

Brown belt drills and conditioning increased in their intensity. Weapons training was also involved throughout the training. The first weapon was taught at the blue belt level and was included up and through the ranks. The sai, nunchaku, kama, tonfa, and bow all added to the difficulty of the training. One never rested. To make a higher rank only meant to be handed a new challenge.

Imagine for a moment being a black belt and watching students rise through the rank. So those with the vaunted rank of *Shodan* or *Nidan,* while training rigorously, were also eyeing students who were coming to get their rank. As a black belt, you were revered, respected, and an obstacle. It was understood that anytime you engaged in sparring or fighting, you would be matched individually against other brown belts or black belts. The real deal.

The rules of engagement while fighting or sparring were as follows: I am speaking as a brown belt or black belt against white or blue belts, upper ranks such as green, brown or black belts are only allowed to use defensive skills. To be offensive against a lower rank is considered destructive to that person's training.

One recollection for me happened on a night when training with two black belts and several other lower ranks. I was a green belt at the time with two stripes soon to be tested for my brown belt. Apparently, the black belts saw that I was progressing well. This necessitated their being ready for sparring. It was a night when I would find great humility in the fight. David and Dale were very strong black belts. The results for them were better than they were for me. After two rounds with them, I ended up with a broken nose and a black eye. Seeing that I was somewhat deflated after having my butt handed to me, both David and Dale were very complimentary of my skills saying that if they had not turned up their fighting skills, I could have beaten them. My day would come.

As I contemplated our fight that night, I realized a very important fact. When you are in tight with someone and you can see the whites of their eyes, you better be blasting, or you would surely be blasted yourself—a valuable lesson that I would take with me throughout the rest of my training.

Anyway, as my training progressed, the rigors of work and

karate took their toll. But I continued to train. It began to be that if you missed class you truly felt that you missed out. The group that I was working with continued to progress so it was important for me to keep up. As I worked through the rank of brown belt toward black, the karate load continued to increase. The training was intense. Blocks, blocks and punches, blocks punches, blocks punches and kicks. Same side, opposite side. All were quite mesmerizing. Add to that the demands of kata and weapons training and it was very necessary to maintain chi. Chi is the energy that is housed in all beings and can even be found in one's home or one's garden.

I found my chi one day while studying with Mr. Ansay. We were involved in a training regimen called "animal circle." Four to six students were positioned around the circle. Each student would deliver one technique upon the calling of his or her number. For example, number one was a straight punch, number two was a snap kick, number three was a thrust kick, and number four was a turning back kick and so on. A student was then chosen for the center of the circle and the drill would begin—one, four, two three, one. The numbers were called in quick succession. The only reprieve being that when your number was called, you allowed the defender one second to prepare.

Eventually, one would become familiar with who was throwing what technique, but it was extremely challenging nonetheless. I remember Mr. Ansay then called for students to get their gear, which meant we would be sparring. With sparring there was a sense of excitement accompanied by a sense of concern for one's well being. After just completing the animal circle drill, I for one, will freely admit that I was getting tired.

As a group, we all started training around the same time so there was some parity in our ability. Fights were going along very well. I guess you could say that there were no major injuries which is always good. As the intensity of the sparring increased, I remember starting to get very tired. When Mr. Ansay realized that I was tiring, he asked another student to step into the ring. I was now fighting multiple attackers. When I realized that I would be fighting two people at the same time, I stepped back and took a huge deep breath. Somehow, from somewhere, I was renewed. I had new-found energy that seemed inexplicable at that moment. I continued to fight and defend myself quite adequately to my great surprise. I'll never forget that moment in my training. It was a valuable lesson and an obvious milestone.

Anyway, I was beginning the final leg of my training for Shodan—first degree black belt. The black belt test consisted of training drills, the performing of 17 kata, and the necessary survival of two rounds of full-contact fighting with two very fresh black belts. It was kind of like waiting to be fed to the lions.

I went through the drills—down straight up blocks, blocks with punches, blocks with kicks, same side, and opposite side—with all eyes upon me. The tension of the test created a tendency to be too tight, too rigid which quickly used up large amounts of energy. Next came the performance of all the kata with full knowledge that any mistakes would necessitate that I redo any particular form which had been done in error. At this point, we're approaching an hour and a half of balls to the wall karate, and fatigue was a heavy weight.

Then the call was made to bow and prepare for sparring. I managed to grab a quick drink and grab my mouthpiece and sparring gloves and return to the center of the dojo. Corey san was chosen to be my opponent for the fighting. He was young, in tremendous physical condition, and would be quite a threat to my survival. Remember in your black belt test you are not expected to win the fight only to survive the fight. Yikes! As we closed ranks, I remember being able to catch Corey with a sneaky left hook that was somewhat of a trademark of mine. But I knew that I would pay, and I did so quickly. As I switched stances, Corey was able to read my body movement and caught me with a vicious snap kick to my lower rib cage on my left side. Immediately I knew that I had broken some ribs and each breath taken after that was extremely painful. Thank God round one ended when it did. Survival of the second round would be extremely difficult, as I was no longer able to catch my breath.

As round two began, I had to fight with my left side back in order to protect my injured ribs. I was unable to generate any offense as I was in too much pain. I was forced into survival mode. Corey made sure to finish any thoughts that I had of getting him back when he caught me with another snap kick inches from my damaged ribs. Down I went. I managed to get up off my knee as the round ended. I never heard a sweeter sound than "yahme" which meant to stop. I was so winded at that moment I fell to my knees and thought I would pass out from the lack of oxygen. After a few moments I was able to catch my breath and I rose to my feet and returned to the center of the dojo.

Sensei Al completed the work of filling out my test form, and much to my delight, he went into a cabinet and came out with my new obi. My new black belt. He bowed and handed it to me, and I bowed and took it from him feeling incredible joy. I turned away from him as was custom and removed my brown belt. I tied my new obi around my waist. I turned back to face sensei and to thank him *–Domo Arigato Sensei*. My pain and fatigue had left me for a moment, but it quickly returned. At the moment, I was reminded of sports scenes that I had seen in the past where people cried with the joy of victory. I cried with that same joy.

One gets to enjoy feeling the accomplishment of making Shodan for just a very short time. In my case it was only a week. The very next Friday at black belt class I was taught new skills and new drills that made me feel like a white belt again. Most victories are short-lived.

I'd like to take a moment to thank Sensei Al Gagne and my brother black belts for their dedication to their training and mine. I still train to this day, and my training has served as a guidepost for my life.

I've explained how I lived so much of my life unsure of myself. My martial arts training was part of the antidote. If you are never sure of yourself in this world, what do you do? I chose not only to fight, but to become a skilled fighter. I chose to pursue freedom over living with fear.

CHAPTER 8

Finding God in the Most Unexpected Places

My relationship with God started with my family at my baptism. I was baptized and raised in the Catholic faith. I attended Catholic schools through the tenth grade. My parents took Peter and me to church on Sundays and my Mom was even a Sunday school organizer during my elementary school years.

My educators were mostly Nuns of the Sacred Heart order with a few lay teachers mixed in during my later elementary years. In the sixth grade, we had a female lay teacher who told us that she had come from overseas after doing missionary work for the Peace Corps. She was a cool teacher, and I had a few of my most enjoyable moments in her class.

But in high school, my faith wandered.

Years later, I found myself living in Sutton, Massachusetts working as a roofing contractor. It was the end of September 2004 and three major hurricanes had devastated the state of Florida over the course of just a few weeks.

I received a call to my office and his message went something like this, "Hello, my name is Bob from Port St. Lucie, Florida." He said that he was originally from Woonsocket, Rhode Island, the city where I grew up, and I actually recognized his name and remembered who he was. His message continued, "Your company has been in the roofing business for many years and I hope you can help us down here in Florida." He left his phone number and I returned his call quickly.

We spoke for a while and it became obvious from our conversation, and from what I had seen on the news, that the devastation in Florida was overwhelming. The resources and manpower were just not available that were needed to handle the vast amount of work to be done. Roofs were the first thing to be destroyed in the storms, followed by immeasurable amounts of water damage to the interior of the buildings, causing damage to both the structures and their contents.

Being a businessman, I understood the opportunity. Being a compassionate man, I understood the need. So, preparations began for me to head to Florida to help with the restoration. I made arrangements with the lead men in our company, packed a bag, loaded ladders on the truck, and off I went. Bob had suggested that I stay at a hotel several hours north of the Port St. Lucie area; however when I got there, there were no hotel rooms available for hundreds of miles north of the disaster area. So I drove on. I arrived at Bob and Linda's house around midnight and being very tired, Bob showed me to a room where I could sleep and I went to bed.

The next morning would bring incredible revelations of utter destruction. I remember one old gent saying that as he flew into the area looking down from the plane, he marveled thinking, "Wow, everyone has a swimming pool down here." But as the plane got closer to the ground, he realized that these were blue tarps covering peoples' roofs—thousands of them.

As Bob and I surveyed the neighborhoods, we saw people gutting the interior of their homes—contents, sheet rock, and furniture—and placing the debris along the side of the road in front of their homes. I would guess millions of tons of debris. Incredible!

Bob and I began to make our plans. God, however, had other ideas.

It bears mentioning at this point that I remember being in Bob and Linda's home those first few days and feeling the presence of our Lord there. And a strong presence it was. Bob is the administrator of the Apostles of Divine Mercy and Linda works in the pro-life movement. God chooses special people to do special things, and these are two very special people. A tear wells up in my eye as I realize what their friendship means to me and how their friendship has changed me.

The need for roofing services in the area was absolutely immense. Bob and I began the task of measuring roofs, and it was all consuming. After a time, a pattern seemed to develop, as the styles of many of the homes were somewhat repetitive. One roof was the same as the roof three houses down and so on. After a while you realize that house number 12 was the same as house number 18 which made estimating much quicker and easier. Before too long we had many estimates ready to produce. People were anxious, as the roof was the first line of defense against the weather. I remember one instance where a homeowner came to Bob's house to seek me out saying, "I hear there's a roofer here from Massachusetts and I need his help."

Things began to fall in place with the distribution companies for material purchases, the necessity of hauling debris, and most importantly the rental of housing for workers who would be following to set-up housekeeping. It would be a grand task. Some of the distribution houses that we used in Rhode Island and Massachusetts were spread down the East Coast, so we seemed to have instant clout with distribution. The same was true with the disposal companies, as some are nationwide. Our good reputation in our home area did bode well for us.

Little did I realize that the true lesson of why I was there still awaited me. We continued our work without travail. Next up was licensing in the state of Florida. I went to the Port St. Lucie town hall, and this was where fate would twist our mission. Necessary paperwork in hand, I approached my turn at the reception desk. Things seemed to be going along smoothly. I was asked to show my insurance information which I produced. The receptionist looked for a moment and a frown appeared on her forehead. She looked up at me and said my liability insurance is fine, but I needed a worker's compensation certificate. I explained to her that she was holding it in her hand, but she said no, it would have to be a certificate issued in Florida.

As I left the town hall, I saw an elderly couple sitting in their car. They seemed quite dejected as they told me of their circumstance. "The town has given us blue tarps to cover our roof, but we have no one to do the work." To this day I carry guilt for not just doing it for them. I was somewhat dejected at my inability to procure a license at that moment, and I just drove away. It's funny the things you remember.

The search to find appropriate insurance would serve as our undoing. We were unable to find anyone willing to write an insurance policy for an out of state roofing contractor despite the fact that the governor of the state of Florida and even the President of the United States had requested contractors like myself to assist in the restoration of the homes in Florida. Our search would prove to be incredibly frustrating. Insurance agents were not returning our calls and the ones that did suggested that they were too busy with their own stuff to be able to do the extensive application process necessary to write a roofing worker's comp policy. That was incredible to believe, because with our help as roofers, agents would have been able to, in turn, help the homeowners.

Calls were made to the governor's office, local officials, senators, and congressman—even to the President of the United States—all for naught. For days on end we answered questions redundantly. The governor's assistant, local officials, assistants from senators and congressmen, even assistants to the presidential campaign (this was right before a presidential election—the incumbent President Bush versus Mr. Kerry). People could not believe our story as we recounted our inability to become insured. Bob and I thought for sure that someone would rise to the occasion and help us get the insurance we needed so we could continue our work to provide estimates for customers.

Finally, we thought we saw a glimmer of hope when a contractor suggested that we work through him to do roofs. Knowing the business very well, I also understood the cost necessary for the job at hand. These contractors turned out to be money-grubbing vultures who suggested that roofing was easy on these one-story Florida homes, and subsequently offered approximately seventy cents on the dollar for us to do the work. Breaking that down, insurance companies in Florida at that time were paying approximately three dollars per square foot for roofing. These contractors were offering two dollars and twenty-five cents per square foot. That boiled down to me doing the work for zero profit. That was not an option.

But there were things that happened during my time with Bob and Linda that were very much in my best interest. God does work in mysterious ways. We came upon a woman who worked in the insurance industry and was willing to enlighten us as to the truth about the Florida insurance market. Sometime before the hurricanes hit Florida, the state insurance commission met to set the rates for insurance costs in the state. She went on to explain that the cost to obtain workers compensation insurance for in-state roofing contractors would be set at approximately $40 per hundred of payroll while the rate for out-of-state contractors would be over $60 per hundred of payroll, thereby closing the door to out-of-state contractors being able to come in during a disaster to lend a hand.

The woman went on to say that she felt that this policy would be unethical and argued against it. At the time, she was involved with the insurance commission. She realized that this may have a devastating effect if outside help were ever needed in an emergency. But the fix was in. I recall that the story even reached the ears of a Fox Television news reporter. He spoke to us daily for a period of three to four days questioning us and then going on to verify what we had told him.

Then came the news that Bob and I would be on Fox News with this reporter to discuss the situation. I remember that it would be a Wednesday when we were to meet him. But early that Wednesday morning the phone rang. Bob answered and all I heard was Bob say, "yes, uh huh, uh huh, okay" and then he hung up.

He looked at me, and I knew there was something wrong. Bob said, "The reporter is not going to do the story." Our fight ended that day, and I knew it was time for me to go home.

We all truly felt that there was a very negative influence at work preventing us from moving forward. We will never know for sure what killed the story, but there were a lot of pressures to keep this issue from coming to light. There were even rumors of mob influence. After all, it's always about the money. I even became a little concerned that I wouldn't make it out of Florida without incident.

Bob and Linda were gracious hosts, and their love of the Lord would end up saving me. I'd be remiss if I didn't tell you how hard the Lord pushed me so that I could find him. During my stay at Bob and Linda's, amidst all the turmoil and confusion, there were two moments that will go down in my mind and in my personal history as key moments that helped save me.

The first moment came on a morning when Bob and Linda had left to attend a funeral. Linda had continually asked me if I had any laundry that needed cleaning and I kept telling her that no, thank you—I would take care of it. I felt awkward putting upon them anymore than my presence in their home already had.

After they had gone out, and without really wanting to look too deeply into cabinets in the laundry room, searched for laundry detergent so that I could wash my dirty clothes. I knelt to look into a cabinet, and with very sore knees, reached onto the counter to pull myself up. I found my hand resting upon a card depicting the mother Mary holding the baby Jesus. The words that came to me at that moment were, *I have been holding you the whole time.*

It immediately struck me that this was a reference to my struggles with adoption and my mistaken thinking that I never had love. I knew right away, at that moment, that this was a message from God and mother Mary. I had been searching for a long time but don't think I ever really took the time to see what I was finding.

This moment was extremely profound for me. It moved me deeply and thoughts of it continues to do so to this day. You see, discovering my biological past would give me a small measure of healing, but the real meaning of life and my own existence was still lost to me.

That very same day, after working out in the driveway performing some martial arts kata, I went into the bathroom to take a shower. Looking into the mirror after shaving, I touched my face and it felt as if it was covered with oil. I wiped my face with a towel and touched it again, but the feeling of an oil-like substance would not go away. I rubbed my hands together and miraculously they were dry. I touched my face again to feel that same oily feeling. I put my face closer to the mirror and my skin looked dry. I rubbed my face again with my hands only to feel that same oily feeling again. I rubbed my hands together again, and they were dry. I was puzzled. I would not realize the significance of that moment until later when I recounted the incident to Bob and Linda.

As we sat for dinner that evening, I told Bob of the two encounters of the day, and they looked at each other and marveled. Finally Linda said, "Brother Paul, it was an anointing." Jesus says, "Take up your cross and follow me." The true meaning of those words is that it's not going to be easy. First mother Mary visits me and soothes me with her words, and then the Lord visits me and anoints me.

We said our goodbyes and I drove away. As I rolled up the highway toward home, it dawned on me that I had been too far away from the Lord for too long. This was illustrated to me by driving over two thousand miles to Florida so that He could find me. I know now that this had been the true purpose of the trip all along. I thank the Lord for finding me. My work will never be done.

CHAPTER 9
Restraint

It has been many years since the incidents in this chapter took place, which is why the writing of this book is long overdue. The meeting which you are about to read about took place sometime in the 1990's. It began in a counselor's office after the demise of my first marriage. The counselor pointed out that I had mentioned on several occasions that I was interested in learning my biological birth history and that now might be a good time to begin the search.

I had known from my parents that I was adopted through the St. Vincent de Paul Society, so I placed a call to the Society to initiate the request for my birth records. The woman who took my call asked me my name and date of birth, and then put my call on hold for a moment. She returned to the call and told me that my records, being from the 1950's, had been placed on microfilm and that it could take several years to retrieve them. She explained that there were many requests for this type of information which created a backlog.

So back to life I went. Several years passed and I found my way into a new relationship. True to form, this relationship also required more than I could give. Was it because I needed to fill the void that I chose women that were a void? I think that if I was always trying to fix them, I didn't have to fix myself.

As I muddled through life with the woman who was to become my second wife, it was a difficult time to say the least. As I look back, I wish that I hadn't thought that I could fix every darn thing. After moving into a new home with wife number two, it wasn't too long after that things blew up and I found myself putting her stuff in the driveway and covering it with a large blue tarp.

Why wasn't I smart enough to see at that moment in my life that this was going to be another thing—another person—who I wouldn't be able to fix? But she was nice enough, and after a while things softened and I brought her stuff back into the house. I was a hopeless idiot thinking that I could create love and romance, and I never allowed myself the notion of failure for very long.

A husband and wife need to have things that you share together, but then there are also times when you need to explore life a little on your own. I took her fishing from time to time, but then if I wanted to go fishing with a friend, she would become jealous and ask why I wouldn't want to fish with her instead. Life is full of ups and downs, good times and bad. It seemed that the good times were only when money was spent on lavish vacations. Otherwise, the anxiety created by an ex-spouse and by the second wife, for a myriad of reasons, was excruciatingly painful.

In one example, my stepchildren's dad stopped at our home to pick up his son for the weekend. The man was so drunk that he instructed his son to drive the truck. The boy was just 13 years old at the time. As the boy drove through the center of our small town, people at the gas station saw him and frantically tracked me down on my cell phone saying, "we just saw the boy driving his dad's truck down Singletary Avenue, and his dad was slumped up against the passenger door of the truck!" I lost it. I called the police and said that I was heading to the father's house where I would be dispatching some justice. The police met me there, and under the very real threat of being arrested, convinced me to go home. My stepson would be brought back to our house by the police. Nothing ever happened to the dad because he was not seen driving the vehicle by a police officer.

Thinking that things would calm down a bit, I proceeded downstairs into my small dojo area to burn off some anxious energy. While I was performing some kata, I heard a loud crash in the driveway in the front of my home. I ran out to see my stepchildren's father's vehicle driving away. I walked out to the street then looked at my truck. The front end was smashed-in and severely damaged. I ran back into the house and throwing on my shoes I said loudly to the kids' mother, "This shit ends tonight!" And off I went chasing after his truck.

As he turned west on to the Central Turnpike, I saw the police slide in behind him. I followed them both to the school bus turnaround on the Oxford town line where he was pulled over. I killed my headlights, and the flashing lights of the police car gave me the cover I needed to pull in behind them unnoticed. I listened to their dad in a drunken stupor trying to justify his actions and plead with the officers to let him go. When I heard that, I stepped out from behind the police car and surprised them all.

I stood there with my bow in hand ready to take them all on just to get to him. When I spoke, he and the officers were completely startled. They had not seen me approach. With the element of surprise in my favor, I offered the two officers a small bribe of $1,000 each to leave me alone with him so I could finish things. One of the officers was a part-timer and said to the officer in charge, "What do you think? Should we take it? I haven't been working much, and I could use the cash." The officers played along with me nicely. If you could have seen the look on the guy's face just then as he began to cry saying to the other officer, "You can't do that! You can't leave me alone with him. He'll kill me!" I promised the officers that I wouldn't hurt him too badly and for them to go to my house and each collect the thousand dollars I had promised. Obviously, the officers couldn't take the money, so I left without realizing my dream of beating his lights out. Oh well.

Just to be fair, here is a bit of my side of the shit song of my life's trials regarding ex's and children. My ex began to see a fellow who my daughter told me had molested her. Picture the angriest person you've ever seen and then multiply that times 100. That was me. We went to the police station, and I sat in the room listening to my little girl, who was ten or twelve at the time, tell the detectives about how she stayed with him one afternoon while mom took her sister to the doctors. "Come sit next to me," he said, and he instructed her to lay on the couch next to him. He began to brush her hair with his hand as he told her what a pretty girl she was. Then he moved his hand around her body while touching her and told her what a pretty girl she was. After hearing that, I walked into the hallway and began to punch a cinderblock wall until my knuckles were bleeding raw. I had an officer friend there named Carl (God rest his soul). When someone said that I should stop punching the wall, Carl told them to leave me alone, that I was okay. Unless you've been through something similar with your child, it is hard to explain the anger, the pain, and the frustration that I felt. I was convinced I would kill the bastard.

There is one lesson I have learned through all this. *You cannot force love, and you cannot fix your way through things that are not meant to be fixed.* My dad told me something a long time ago.

I remember he once said, "When I yelled at your mom one day and then saw how sad I made her feel, I promised to myself that I would never make her feel that way again." That people—is love.

The police opened an investigation and it ended up being heard by a grand jury in a courthouse in Providence, Rhode Island. The grand jury ruled that it was a "he said she said case," and without any real proof of an assault, they would not bring charges. What was I going to do to avenge this wrong? I had to do something.

As luck would have it, I was on a particular street in my old hometown looking for a house that I was contacted to measure for a new roof. I suddenly saw the guy walking along the sidewalk, but he didn't recognize me in the truck right away. When I got up close to him, I called out his name and said, "God has delivered you to me!"

I'll never forget the look of fear on his face and in his eyes as he ran to the closest house, and banged on the door and screamed, "Help! Call the police! He is going to kill me!"

A woman opened the door. I enjoyed watching the little bastard squirm as he waited for the police to arrive, and I also enjoyed the look on his face when the officer got there. It was my buddy Carl. This was one of God's little rewards to me. To make it official, Carl questioned me about what I was doing there, and I honestly told him that I was looking for a house to measure a roof. Then Carl turned and looked at the woman who answered the door and said, "Now I don't know what this fellow's problem is, but this guy is a businessman just looking for a house to measure a roof." And away he drove.

Before Carl proceeded to drive away, he said to me, "Don't hurt him too badly."

Then I smiled back at the diddler and asked him, "So… what are you going to do now? How fast can you run?"

I watched this guy run through backyards and jump fences as I drove along the street watching this piece of shit try to escape the beating that he knew was coming.

But as much as I wanted to, I knew I couldn't hurt him because I needed to be around for my children. So that day I had to put his fate in God's hands. I had no choice but to let God forgive him or not. It was out of my hands. Would I have beaten him if I had caught him? I wonder if the real question is would I have been able to stop? Thankfully, I will never know.

CHAPTER 10
"It's you, isn't it?"

Then one day a message came in from the St. Vincent de Paul Society. My birth records were available for me to review. I called them back to set up an appointment, and the lady asked if I would like to have a counselor sit with me while I read the report. I was pretty sure that I could handle whatever it is I was going to learn, at least for the moment anyway. How true that thought turned out to be.

As I drove to the appointment, I would be lying if I said that I wasn't a bit nervous. My whole life raced through my thoughts. I was frozen in that moment.

We met and introduced ourselves. We sat at a small round table in the corner of the main room. She handed me a piece of paper and there was my life—in the beginning. There were a few sentences on the paper that read something like this… *"She was a red-haired lady who taught elementary school. He had come a few years later to find me, but they would give him no information as to my whereabouts."*

That was it? That's all there was! She seemed to apologize at the lack of information, and I offered her my thanks anyway as I walked away. As I got in my truck and started the drive home,

I was thinking of what was to be the next step in my search… if there would be a next step at all. Life would go back to being life I supposed, but for now I had these few new tidbits of information that I could toss around in my mind.

It was another rainy day, and I found myself sitting alone in my dad's green vinyl recliner next to the telephone, set on a small table with a lamp hanging from a turned wooden post. In those next few moments, God seemed to take the wheel. In my possession, I had my birth certificate that said I was born in Burrillville, Rhode Island in March of 1955. And the Society had told me my mother had been an elementary school teacher with red hair. I didn't see how this tidbit was useful or relevant, then I had a sudden thought.

I picked up the phone and searched for the phone number to the Burrillville School Department. I dialed the number and an elderly woman answered. I said, "Ma'am, it sounds by your voice that you may have worked at the Burrillville School Department for many years." She replied in a voice that I can easily mimic to this very day, "all my life." (You know, as I just typed those words, I spoke them mimicking her voice!)

I continued and said, "Ma'am, I am looking for a woman—a schoolteacher—with red hair who may have left school for a while to have a child in early 1955."

Without a moment's hesitation, she responded, "It could only have been one of two people. One of those woman passed away some time ago, and the other woman's last name was Lace, but now I believe it is Johnson."

With another call to information, I asked for the number of any Johnson family living in Pascoag, Rhode Island. I was given one number, and taking a deep breath, I made the call. I remembered that years ago when I asked my dad what happened to my biological mother, he told me she had passed away. I didn't believe this was the truth. I knew this is what many parents were instructed to tell their children if ever they were to ask of the whereabouts of their biological parents.

Ring... ring... ring... and then a woman answered the phone. I asked for Mr. Johnson and she hesitated before stating, "I'm sorry but Mr. Johnson has passed away. I am Mrs. Johnson. Is there something I can help you with?"

At that moment I realized that I could be speaking to the woman who I had wondered about for my entire life. I asked, "Ma'am, are you sitting down?" She hesitated and said yes. I then asked her, "Did you leave school in early 1955 to have a child?"

After a short pause she said, "It's you, isn't it?"

"Yes," I said. "It very well could be."

My heart was pounding in my chest. We chatted a bit and I asked her for her address. I told her I would call before I stopped by.

When I hung up the phone, I began to cry—a cleansing cry that seemed to last for hours and hours. I can't even remember if I told anyone about this as I planned out the forthcoming meeting in my mind. It wasn't long after that brief conversation, maybe a day or two, that I made the ride from where I had grown up in Woonsocket, Rhode Island to where she lived in Pascoag, Rhode Island—*just fifteen miles!*

That was it. It turns out that my whole life, I searched for someone that was so close by all that time.

It was raining when I turned into her driveway. I sat in the truck for a while seemingly frozen in time. I can still recall looking into a puddle in the driveway and seeing the rain drops as they fell and hit the water. I wondered if I was doing the right thing, but I had come too far to turn back now. It took me a few minutes before I could get myself out of the truck. As I walked around the back of the vehicle, a young man came jogging down a few stairs to greet me. He looked up at me and said, "Hey! So you must be my big brother!"

We stood there for a while giving each other a hug while standing in the rain. He confided in me that his birth certificate stated, "child number two," so he always wondered but never dared to ask. Maybe, he said, it was that he didn't want to know. He said that he thought that maybe his mom had a child who passed away. Then he said that we should go inside, as Mom has been waiting anxiously. We walked into the house, and that was when I first laid eyes on her.

She was sitting in "her chair" as my new brother AJ would later call it. She suffered from poor vision and asked me to come closer so she could see me better. She stood up to give me a hug and grabbing me on both sides of my face by my beard, she pulled me in close and said, "I've been waiting a long time to look into those eyes." As she stood, I could see she was a short little Irish lady with curly hair, who had been dealing with diabetes and its effects for many years.

We sat and talked for a while, but I think we were both in shock at the reality of what was happening. I can't remember if it was Beth or Ellen who walked into the room next, but it was one of my new sisters who came in and said that she saw AJ's car in the driveway and wanted to see what was up. She lived in a small apartment that adjoined the house. At that moment, she was introduced to her older brother. We were equally stunned at the news. After a little small talk, I said my goodbyes and was off to return home and mull over what had just happened.

I will never forget what she looked like in that moment. And I never saw her again. It was just a few years after that meeting that she passed away. There were reasons why I never saw her again, which I will try to explain.

In one phone conversation after our meeting, the subject of

birthdays came up. I said mine was on March 30th, but she said no, that's not correct. She continued that she no longer remembered the real date. I thought to myself, *you couldn't remember the day I was born?* It turns out that the date, March 30th, was the date that I was brought to the orphanage.

She began to write me letters and signed them, "Love Mom." I decided I would have none of that, as I considered my true mom and dad to be the people who adopted and raised me. My mom and dad were alive at the time I met her and it seemed to bother my mom that she may have been supplanted. I was quick to reassure her saying, "Come on Ma, you're my mom!" In hindsight, I thank God for that moment because my behavior through the years was never a sign of thanks to the parents that afforded me this incredible life. I will always be very thankful to them from the bottom of my heart. A portrait of my mom and dad, painted in the early 1960's, still hangs over the mantel above my fireplace to this very day.

Even after all those years of searching and scanning the crowds, finding my birth mother didn't change things the way I thought they would. The experience only put the onus back on me. I realized it didn't matter. It didn't change any of the mistakes I made in my life. I realized that those things I was searching for, I had all the time. It turns out that the person I had really been looking for all those years was right there all along looking back at me in the mirror.

I'd like to share a few tidbits about how small the world really is. One day, I went to my daughter Julia's field hockey game to watch her play. As I stood there and cheered her on, some younger children came up to me to say hello and go on to say that they were cousins of mine. Then a few adults came over and introduced themselves saying they were cousins, too.

Another time I had been called to come and give a customer

a price for a roof. I went out to meet with them and we sat and talked about the project. It was a new construction home, so we discussed the product and timeline for installation. My company did the job, and all went well. Twenty-five years later, my brother AJ would comment, "How could you not see the resemblance? You guys are like twins!" It turns out those customers were my Uncle Jack and Aunt Terry. I had unknowingly sat across the table from my aunt and uncle but did not see the resemblance. Imagine that if you can.

At the beginning of the first chapter of this book, you may recall I told the story of a hot summer day long ago when I was working on a porch roof in Pascoag. I struck up a conversation with a pretty young girl as I worked, and nearly walked off the job and slipped through her window to what all young men like to do (or at least want to do). I'm thankful to this day that I needed the money more than a good time, and that I chose to stay on the roof that day and finish the job. Many years later, I would meet that curly-haired girl again. It was my sister Ellen. Think about that one for a while.

As life went on, my everyday struggles would remain. What began as a quest for knowledge of self overwhelmed me. I had a family, I thought, but here came a whole other one. And although I had wanted and thought about this my entire life, I must admit I was still not prepared for what it all would mean to me.

Epilogue

As I ponder the story of my life, including all the trials, tribulations and a few good things mixed in to help keep me sane, I wish to offer a message to adopted children and foster children to help them deal with their own questions.

Through every moment of my life, I never gave up the will to succeed. You can't either. Everything I did was lost somehow in the belief that I needed to know who I was. The reality came to me only after many years and a long journey back to my faith. I'm not sure what it will take for you to achieve that comfort, but I hope this story helps you in some way. Don't go chasing rainbows that you'll never find the end of. And if you do find the end, be prepared—you might find there won't be a pot of gold when you get there.

Look at yourself in the mirror instead. That person in the mirror is who you really need to discover. Set some goals. Find those things that you like to do and become good at them. Learn everything you can when you are young, because life comes along fast, wraps you up, and takes you for a ride whether you want to go or not. If you're not prepared for the ride, it will be bumpy.

Stay away from the things that you know can hurt you and that you do not understand. If you don't know yourself, how can you expect to figure out anyone else? If you're lucky enough to be in a relationship with someone who loves you and who you love right back, work out a way to give time to each other. Enjoy the things that you both enjoy, and don't be envious or intolerant of your spouse or significant other. Try to enjoy something that is not your cup of tea so to speak. Allow each other the time to enjoy the things that each of you enjoy and don't smother each other. I cannot tell you exactly how to work this balance, but what I can tell you is that if you don't try, you will fail. There are no good excuses for losing. When you lose, you lose. There are no valid excuses that will make losing okay. You can run around a field picking up all the bullshit that you can find, but no one will want any. Besides, the bull may chase you and that won't be any fun.

The struggles that I've endured throughout my life feel like grains of sand on a beach. There are so many. Individual struggles will come and go, so don't worry so much about the who, what, when, where, or why… just take care of that person you see in the mirror. Although some you might have to look for, and some will appear over time, the answers are sure to come. Don't push it. If you push too hard, you end up pushing people away.

The lessons that I've learned are contained in the pages of this book. If you can make my struggles yours and then avoid them, I think you can succeed. The years between finding my biological mother and sitting down to write this story have all been necessary. Becoming me was a lifetime endeavor. You can make it easy, or you can make it difficult. The choice is yours. But by hearing my story, I do hope yours becomes easier.

In the beginning of this book somewhere I wrote about my first love. She was then and she is now, after 40 years, the love of my life. And she is in my life again. I can hear her laughing in the other room as she talks to her friend on the phone. The sound of her laughter is a joyous sound. I never gave up. I never stopped trying, and I have found my one true love.

Maybe that will be my next story… or maybe yours in your story.

###

About the Author

Paul Mainville has lived his life full-on.

Trials and tribulations, highs and lows—call them whatever you like, through it all he showed the courage to persevere.

In business he has shown honesty and integrity, which are the cornerstones of his personal and professional success.

Faith in God, martial arts training, and knowledge of Native American tradition have all formed the man that he is today.

This book is a culmination of his life up to this point.

www.ingramcontent.com/pod-product-compliance
Lightning Source LLC
Chambersburg PA
CBHW022108040426
42451CB00007B/185